Forest Leaves

A selection of poems by

Marigold Pritchard

TO ARTHUR
I hope you will enjoy this book,
Companion to "Forest Folo"
Best wishes
Marigold.

Fineleaf Editions, 2009
www.fineleaf.co.uk

Dedicated to my husband, John, for all his hard work helping
me to prepare the manuscript, and to my son, Christopher
and my grandson, William.

First edition © 2009 Marigold Pritchard
ISBN 978-0-9557577-6-1

Design: Philip Gray
Text: Bembo
Print: SS Media
Cover image: Klikk
Forest Stewardship Council certified paper

Published by Fineleaf Editions 2009
Moss Cottage, Pontshill, Ross-on-Wye HR9 5TB
www.fineleaf.co.uk
books@fineleaf.co.uk

British Library Cataloguing in Publication Data
A catalogue record for this book is available from the British Library

CONTENTS

INTRODUCTION

I WAS BORN AT SPEECH HOUSE in the Forest of Dean in the 1930's, during the depression. I was the youngest of three daughters of Clem and Nellie Weager. My sisters Joan, Diana and I were nicknamed respectively Pip, Squeak and Wilfred.

Speech House Cottages

We were very lucky that we were given lots of love and protectiveness from devoted parents. In those days we were fortunate to be able to roam freely and play safely in the Forest.

Diana, Joan and Marigold (R) Speech House, 1955

Although I am visually impaired, and have been for some years now, I try not to let it interfere with my writing but obviously some days are better than others, which also applies to the condition Fibromyalgia from which I also suffer. I feel that I can express myself through poetry and I derive great satisfaction when I have finished a poem.

Some of my poems are from personal experience but others are purely from my imagination. My family, who encourage me in my writing, are very supportive, especially my grandson William who suggests some of the ideas for my poetry. I lose myself when I am writing and am oblivious to what is going on around me. I have always had a love of reading since a child.

In 2008 I wrote a poem as a tribute to HM Queen Elizabeth II and sent it to her. To my delight I received a reply from Buckingham Palace thanking me for the poem and for the sentiments expressed in my verses.

During the 1970's my husband our son and I went to visit my sister and her family in the beautiful State of Kentucky in the USA for one month. My sister lived in the country which comprises woods and valleys so like the Forest of Dean it was unbelievable. We had a very enjoyable and happy reunion, but were glad to come home; the climate was very hot and humid. We missed the greenness of England. My Sister had met an American serviceman who was stationed in the Forest of Dean during World War II and consequently became a GI bride, moving to America as a young bride after the war.

I still believe our beautiful Forest of Dean is the best place in the world in which to live, and I consider it a privilege to have been born a Forester.

Marigold Pritchard
Coleford, June 2009

BATTLE OF WILLS

THE BELL HAS RUNG, it's time for class
Hopefully the day will pass
Without too much disruption and interruption
From the kids assembled here today
It's like trying to keep the enemy at bay.

You're not allowed to touch the little dears
But sometimes how I long to run amok with a pair of shears
I'd soon cut them down to size
And let them see the whites of my eyes
To show them that I'm no soft touch
But my knuckles are white round the ruler I clutch
I mean to get the upper hand
I'll break up their little band.

There's a pistol sound as books are dropped upon the floor
It's nothing new, they've done it before
They think they'll wear me down but I've been round the track
So many times I've met myself coming back
Heaven alone knows what they'll be like in ten years time
If they survive
They're bad enough now and they're still only five.

TO A SOLDIER

THINK NOT OF THE TIREDNESS and the fatigue
Just remember you're one of many of the human league
Sent to battle against a common foe
Knowing that sometimes it is a hard row to hoe
And there is no shame if a tear should fall
When the loss of a comrade is felt by all
You have to soldier on my friend
And pray that this war will come to an end.

While the politicians duck and dive
Just concentrate on trying to stay alive
Do not be distracted by thoughts outside your sphere
Keep in mind what is now and here
Wear your uniform with pride
And let your conscience be your guide.

Think of the speech at Agincourt that Henry V gave to his men
Which gave fresh heart when they were feeling low
And inspired them to give the enemy a blow
You can do the same we know
For of your bravery and courage no one can deny
For men have e'er been sent to die
So we pray for your safe return
While we wonder what its all for
The futility of war.

THE WISH

HE SAT THERE deep in concentration
Patiently waiting, paying attention
His young face unlined, well deep in thought
As from time to time he cast an eye over what he'd brought.

His mother had packed him a special lunch
He'd picked out a sandwich and begun to munch
Then suddenly his excitement rose
He forgot his cold feet as he wriggled his toes.

He jumped to his feet and reeled in his line
A beaming smile on his face like warm sunshine
For Billy had achieved his dearest wish
He had caught his first fish.

THE BIRTHDAY

I LOOK FORWARD to my birthday
In fact I do so every year
Perhaps this time it will be different
But I don't hold out much hope I fear
It has arrived at last
Will it improve on birthdays past?

I had a pair of gloves hand knitted from my gran
They were multi-coloured and when washed the colours ran
Some smellies from the aunties
And from my true love some sexy panties
They do say love is blind
The size he bought were tiny they didn't fit my large behind.

My mother bought me tonic wine
Because I looked 'rather peaky'
She said the bags beneath my eyes
Made me look quite freaky.

The children bless them gave me chocs
And some one else gave me a sewing box
Never mind it's the thought that counts
And on that note I'll bow out with a flounce.

TO MY DEAR LOVE

Y OU'VE WALKED BESIDE ME since first we met
We seemed to gel, a pattern was set
You are my helpmate, lover, companion and best friend
And also my rock and a willingness to lend
A sympathetic ear when my problems seem to build
From little molehills to mountains and my fears are stilled.

Your loving arms surround me which makes me feel secure
And soothe and comfort me for what I have there is no cure
So I bless the day I met you I'm sure that it was meant
And as I look at your dear face I feel a warm content.

WHEN YOU ARE YOUNG

WHEN YOU ARE YOUNG you never think you will grow old
When you are young the years slip by
And you find the ageing years are cold
When you are young you meet the years with laughter in your heart
And never think how soon will youth depart.

When old age gives you lots of time to ponder on
And wonder where the years have gone
Then say "I wish I'd never taken youth for granted
When I could walk for miles and never panted".

Now I find the stairs too much for my old legs
And find that life has left me with the dregs
So make the most of youth while it's still yours
For you will soon be found behind the old age doors
And then you'll know that you've grown old.

NO OTHER PLACE

THERE IS NO OTHER PLACE when we pass on
Only memories remain for our loved ones when we are gone
No pearly gates with St. Peter waiting in the wings
Nor welcome from a Heavenly Host which sings
Just fairy tales to comfort those behind on earth
Where we try to lead a blameless life while here for
What it's worth.

We leave behind memories to help us through the pain
Of knowing that we won't be here to live again
Memories and dreams are all that is left behind
For us to muse upon and occupy the mind
And while away the lonely hours behind closed door
Waiting for our spirit to lift and soar
And heal the bruised heart until no more.

THE VISIT

THERE'S A CARE HOME for the elderly not very far from me
The family think I should try it 'just to see'
To see what I ask myself meditatively,
Do they want to get rid of me and shirk all responsibility
For my immediate and future needs.
I've heard the matron is dressed in twinsets and in tweeds
She sounds a right old dragon and not my sort at all
The home sounds very posh, it's called 'the Hall'.

Perhaps I ought to investigate and see what it has to offer
I'll wear my fur coat and my pearls which I keep in a velvet lined coffer
I should look my best when all is said and done
I don't want her to think I'm a time waster looking for fun.
I had to make an appointment, no going there on 'spec'
Have they something to hide I ask at the door
And I watch the receptionist go pink at the neck
She retorts stiffly, "Not at all."

The day has arrived I am going to view
I am told the Hall only takes a few
On a one-to-one basis the staff are employed
No wonder it's expensive, I'm not overjoyed.
I'm shown a large bedroom, tidy and neat
I'm told that the room is also en-suite
The Dining room is next with tables all laid
And vases of flowers all neatly displayed.

Then its the lounge where the residents sit
In chairs round the room no faces are lit
With interest or animation it seems.
Some are dozing, perhaps sunk in their dreams
It all looks depressing they are waiting for god
There's a smell from the kitchens the aroma of cod.

I thank the matron for showing me around
And she smiles graciously and hopes that I have found
The viewing satisfactory and I smile back and say
I haven't decided but may come back some day
I couldn't wait to get home to a strong G and T
Me? Go into a Home? Not Pygmalion likely.

THE HUNTERS

THE NIGHT WAS COOL with a dampish feel
An owl screeched in the gathering dusk
Swooping in search for his evening meal
The smell of the fox on the air like musk
As he travelled abroad, his intent to steal.

Little creatures rustled in the undergrowth
Disturbing grass and leaves
Trying to avoid a common foe
As they scurried and hurried through the evening breeze.

A bat glided across the skyline
Caught in the light of the rising moon
Making the most of the shadowy evening
For daylight comes all too soon.

THE SURPRISE

SALLY WAS ASLEEP and dreaming
As she lay the sun came streaming
Through the window brightly dancing
Cutting 'cross her sleep and lancing
Any thoughts of slumber deep.

She slowly surfaced eyelids heavy
As through her fingers she did peep
At a little figure by the bedside
With a beaming smile from ear to ear
She hadn't heard him coming near.

And said, "What are you doing here my dear?"
He said, "I've brought a cup of tea for you Dad."
She gazed owlishly at the little lad,
"Where did you get the water from?"
She asked this little soul
He smiled so proudly and replied,
"Why! From the doggies bowl."

THE SKY

I LOOK UP and see a mackerel sky
They say that means the weather will be neither wet nor dry
And when the rippling clouds have changed their mind
We see a pattern of a different kind.

A light wind springs up forming clouds into unusual shapes
Another time they look like hanging drapes
Sometimes they look like islands in a sea of azure blue
The sky can also turn quite threatening and of a darker hue.

The facets of the universe which fascinate the eye
To show us how different aspects maketh up the sky
We marvel at the picture which lies above our heads
And of all the various colours of whites to pinks and reds
The sky never stays the same although it's constant there
To let us as mere mortals know that its talents it will share.

MY DAD

MY FATHER didn't believe in diplomacy and tact
At speaking his mind he was a real class act
He spoke straight from the shoulder
He never learnt discretion even as he got older.

My mother used to cringe at the way he spoke his mind
He didn't suffer fools gladly or pull his punches mind
But he had a heart of gold and did many a good turn
And we were proud of him really although our ears would burn
At comments he would make to who upset him
And would quickly strike at the slightest whim.

My father's been gone now for many a year
But I sometimes fancy that I feel him near with his teasing laugh and face so dear
I expect he's telling St Peter a thing or two
And still embarrassing mum, well that's nothing new
I'm sure she joined him to supervise his pranks
I miss them both but for the happy years they gave me I give thanks.

PROFUNDITY

CHILDREN HAVE NO ARTIFICE
They speak straight from the heart
Their little minds unfettered right from an early start
They never see the colour of other children's skin
They only see a kindred spirit and friendship from within.

If only some adults felt the same and put prejudice behind them
What pleasure they would feel and see that we sing from the same anthem
For children can teach us a lesson there is no doubt
So look within yourselves and push the demon out.

The world would be a better place if we thought like children do
And followed their example and saw it through
It sounds so simple, if only this were true
But it may prove difficult so just start with a few
And watch it grow and grow and grow
We live in hope, but you never know
For miracles can happen, they are round us every day
For someone, somewhere, there is always time to pray.

LADIES WHO DO

THERE ARE LADIES who do and ladies who don't
Ladies who will and ladies who won't
And ladies who give a flat no,
There are ladies who'll oblige for the right remuneration
And you'll find this can apply right across the nation
So don't forget to tip your hat and bow.

So if you're feeling rather desperate and can't find one who'll come across
You're not alone in this situation and feeling the sad loss
Of the daily help, that national treasure who came to people's aid
There used to be an army of them, the pinafore brigade.

OLD AGE

OLD AGE is when you're living in the past
Trying to forget, for now, winter's icy blast
Remembering the days when we basked in the warmth of the sun.
When we enjoyed many days of fun
When blood ran hot throughout young veins
Through summer's suns and winter rains.

Old age means wearing thermal vest
To protect our very vulnerable chests,
From bitter winds and frost filled air
For we know that old age means taking care.

We reminisce and go down memory lane
And say that life was different years ago
We wear rose coloured glasses and see the past with a rosy glow
Some things were better there's no doubt
But there were also times when lots of people went without
We have to accommodate the present mode of life
For that is all we've got
So we'll have to grin and bear it and accept our lot.

NOW I'M A WIDOW

WHY IS IT that now I'm a widow
Things aren't the same I fear
I used to be half of a couple when my husband was here.

We had lots of friends, or so I thought
But now some friendships have come to nought
The wives appear to think that I'm a threat
And that I'll lure their husbands into my net Now I'm a widow.

It's lonely being a widow and I hate being so alone
I know I've still got the family but they've all got lives of their own
They visit me often and chat on the phone
And sometimes take me out
But you can't turn the clock back I'm sorry to say
Or I'd have my husband back any day
Now I'm a widow.

I've joined the local bereavement club
For they've all gone through it like me
I hoped it would be some solace in like minded company.

It's no problem leaving the house I find
It's when I return for there's no one to mind
To ask what sort of a day have I had and who I've seen
Well, you'll know what I mean If you're a widow.

TIME

WHAT IS TIME?
Time is relevant
It can slip by
In the twinkling of an eye.

When we are early for an appointment
We hang about
We say that we are killing time
On occasions we'd like to do this literally no doubt.

Time is as unyielding as rock
And inexorable as it doth mock
As against it's power we try to pit
Our puny efforts to defy it.

But it wins the race every time
For it is greater than man,
That's why it is called Time.

I'M A FORESTER

I WAS BORN in the forest
And I am a Forester through and through,
Born in a cottage 'cause hospitals births were few.

If you cut me I'm sure that green sap you would see
Instead of red blood you might expect of me,
For the life's blood of the Forester pumps my heart
Thus where ever I've travelled I've come back to the start.
For the forest is like a magnet drawing me home
Where I feel safe and secure when I've finished my roam.

Yes! I'm a Forester through and through,
True to my roots and if you're a Forester that includes you,
So don't let modernity water the blood in your veins
But stand up and be counted and accept the gains
Of staying true to yourself and the pride that is seen
In being a Forester in our beautiful Forest of Dean.

THE HOMECOMING

SHE CAME UP THE DRIVE, the gravel crunched beneath her feet
The noise sounded loud and her heart began to beat,
And thud inside her head
With every step and tread.
The house looked most unfriendly with windows large and bleak.
She gave a mental shake of the head although her legs felt weak.

Was that someone breathing behind the door
She thought as her key went in the lock.
At this her knees began to knock
And her spirits sank to the floor
A shiver ran down her back from the fear she could not hide
For the house was all in darkness
And ghosts stood by her side.

And suddenly lights were blazing, there were people all around
"Surprise! Surprise!" they all shouted and she found
That she was smiling with sheer pleasure
And thought this moment I will treasure
As they all chorused "Happy Birthday" for good measure.

FIRST DAY

HE STARTED SCHOOL in his fifth year
Did he like it? No fear
He ran away three times before the morning break
Each time I took him back it made my heart ache
To see the misery in his face as I took him through the gate
I thought perhaps he'll settle now but I'll just wait
To see if he makes another dash to leave the class.

I say to him, "The day will soon pass
And I'll be here to pick you up and we'll have egg and chips for tea"
At this his little face lights up
He turns a tear stained face and smiles at me
And I say, "Bye bye love, see you. at three."

A CHRISTMAS GATHERING

COME IN, have a glass of sherry
What! You've had two or three already
Well it doesn't hurt to be merry
As Bob Cratchett said my dear
Christmas comes but once a year.

Have a drink of tea
There's nothing quite like a cup of Rosie Lee
No! Of course you won't spoil your lunch
If on a mince pie or two you munch.

We have Aunty Jo and Uncle Phil
He'll be moaning about his health still
But he'll be lost among the crowd
For talking about ill health is not allowed.

Who would have thought we'd have snow for Christmas Day
The children were out early to make a snowman while the snow still lay
I gave them Dad's old hat and scarf.
It's good to hear the children laugh
The fresh air will do them the world of good
And they'll be from under my feet as they should.

Yes, we've got mistletoe hanging in the hall
For our Jim likes to catch them all
Young and old alike he doesn't discriminate
He even kissed the vicar once who came calling rather late
Our Jim said cheerfully, "I catches 'em all vicar
Who comes sailing through our gate."

The turkey's roasting in the oven, the Christmas pudding's steaming
And when the vegetables are done the potatoes will need creaming
There's such a lot to do my dear and no time for dreaming
I've got more pastry to roll out for apple tart's a favourite
And I've worked out where everyone is to sit
I must keep uncle Phil away from our Fred who thinks he's a bit of a wit

There's fresh cream trifle in the fridge already for the table
That reminds me some one's missing has anyone seen Mabel?
Oh! She's down the garden picking sage ready for the stuffing
With her old dog following behind a panting and a puffing.

Let's see, how many are here to stay to eat
There's Sue and Jack, Aunty Jo and Uncle Phil
Fred and Mabel and also young Will
And me of course and my old man
Plus Sue and Jack's two kids and you and Stan
Oh Dear! That makes thirteen in all
Now let me think. Great Aunt Maud said she might call
I'll send our Fred to fetch her here.

I know she's fond of festive cheer
And she likes the kids, that's a good job
I expect she'll slip them a couple of bob
Well well that's a relief
I'd better take a look at the beef
Everything seems to be going smoothly I must say
So let's get on and enjoy a real family Christmas Day.

ROUGH DIAMOND

WHAT DO YOU THINK of Mrs. Jones ol' but
Hers got a lodger and his appetite's so big he da yut and yut and yut
He's yut her out of house and wum and is costing her a mint
And they do soy that his eyes be queer and that he's also got a squint
Thoust con't tell if him's looking at you or the mon across the street
He da look real rough and a right dead beat.

I tell yuh ol' but he real gives me the creeps
But her seems to like un heaps and heaps
She da look fondly at un while the family all complain
That they da find his presence quite a pain
He da take up much of her time and they don't want him around
After all their pressure she da give in and thic dog is sent back to the pound.

FOR I'M NOT ONE TO GOSSIP

I'M NOT ONE TO GOSSIP as you know
But those new people at number nine
Well, she's always got washing on the line
My Jim wishes she'd give it a miss once in a while
Saying this with a rueful smile
He likes to get a good bonfire on the go
But there's always a lineful on show
But there I'm not one to gossip as you know.

Do you think there's something going on at number eight
There's always people coming and going through their gate
Delivery men mostly and calling very late
But it doesn't do to speculate
For I'm not one to gossip as you know.

What about those kids at number ten
Their mother clucks after them like some old hen
What can you expect when their dad ran off you see
With that brazen piece who lives at number three
It must have been a shock and a terrible blow
But I'm not one to gossip as you know.

And what about her at number five
She's so timid, she looks barely alive
I hear he beats her black and blue
On Saturday nights when he's had a few
He's a bully and a coward, the lowest of the low
But there, I'm not one to gossip as you know.

And then there's him at number seven
His wife is years younger than him
He must be in seventh heaven
Chucked his first wife so I'm told
Said that she was far too old
But I'm not one to gossip as you know.

Then there's that lazy girl who lives at number one
I'm surprised that she gets any house work done
Chats to all the tradesmen knocking at the door
Hello! That's a new one I haven't seen him before.

Quite good looking if you like that sort of course
He's dressed in a blue uniform must be from the force.
Well I can't stand her all day I've got my work to do
Or I'll never finish in time to make a brew
To sit and chat to our new rep
I don't know how you find the time to gossip on the step
I really don't, so cheerio
For I'm not one to gossip as you know.

FAIR SABRINA

BEAUTIFUL SABRINA heading for the sea
Now known as the Severn flowing to the estuary
What secrets does she hide beneath her dark and murky depth
Sunken treasure, gold perhaps, along her length and breadth
Roman coins may yet be found if a diver cares to look
But care should be taken where he treads
For there is many a treacherous nook.

The river can be smooth as glass and idly lap upon its shores
But in the Spring it can be fierce as adventurous folk ride upon it's bores
The elvers pose a challenge to the fishermen who come there
And cause some disappointment for the nets are sometimes bare.

The river has a fascination for young and old alike
But if they decide to swim they'd better watch out for a pike
Who is very antisocial and doesn't like to share his patch
But with a fisherman's rod and line he can meet his match
So the river goes on about its business
Caring for none on its way to the sea
 Hiding all its secrets from you and me.

A LOST CAUSE

THEY SAY THAT I'M BOOZER, well maybe this is so
But I know when I've had a drink or two I feel a rosy glow,
And I feel a sense of well being as I look at the world around.
What's that moving beneath my feet why I do declare it's the ground.

I must have had more to drink than I thought
I think I had better lie down
I feel quite fragile I must admit as I stagger towards my bed,
Oh! I wish some one would stop this merry-go-round
It's doing things to my head.

The family all say that I'm killing myself and the doctor he agrees too
I wish they'd give over, I really do
And I think of all this as I nurse my hangover
Believe me this is nothing like being in clover.

Why now I've had a sleep I feel so much better except my head's in a fog
Well perhaps another drink will cure that
So I'll have a hair of the dog.

A COSY CHAT

"COME IN, SIT DOWN and rest your back
I'll make a cup of tea and we'll have a crack
How are you my dear?
I haven't seen you much this year."

"Well no, my arthritis has been painful
It's like being on the rack
And we've had problems with our Jack."

"Oh yes, I hear he's been a bit of a lad
Not like you or his dad
Time he settled down with a young lass
But he's always had plenty of sass
And how's your Jenny since the new baby was born
Is that two or three now? She must be fair worn."

"Oh our Jenny is fine and bonny now
Although she complains of being a milch cow
They say breast is best the midwives voice
When we were young no one had much choice."

"And Mary? I hear she has a new young man
Is he okay? Do you like him?"
"He's alright I suppose. A bit of an also ran
Not like the last one full of vim and vigour
Always up the gym 'watching his figure'
Our Mary said she'd rather he'd watched hers
And beside he was mean, kept his money in a purse."

"Young Sam has a new sports car or so I'm told
Let me top up your tea before it gets cold."
Sarah drunk up her tea and rose to leave
Pushing back her chair.
"I'll have to get back, my Stan's in bed
As Shakespeare says 'Knitting up the ravelled sleeve of care'."

Her companion reached up to where the rent book was kept on the shelf
Beside a blue vase which looked like Delft.
Sarah said, "It's nice to be back doing my old job
But I'm afraid your rent's gone up a few bob.
Well good bye Jim see you next week if not before."
As the old man walked with her to the door.

THE TABLES TURNED

WHY IS IT when you ring your kids and ask of them a favour
It's "does it have to be right now?" and they hum and haw and haver
But when the boot's on the other foot that's a different flavour
They wheedle and cajole and want it ASAP
They'll even settle for like yesterday, it does appear to me.

Why are parents so vulnerable when it comes to kids demands
We bend over backwards so it seems and perform several mental hand stands
We spoil them rotten so its all our fault
And we find it very difficult to halt
The pattern of giving in.

For peace and quiet to say to each other
That's the penalty for being a father and a mother
And when they're married with kids of their own
We'll show no sympathy for when they moan
That the kids keep them waiting for things to be done
We'll say with heart felt fervour, "welcome to the club my son".

THE PRODIGAL

MY SISTER is my parents favourite, the apple of their eye
They talk about her all the time although she rare comes by
Then one day a letter lands upon the front hall mat.
As I enter through the door they say "No time to chat
Our Susan's coming home my dear."
And I see mum shed a tear
"She's been away such a long time," they cry,
"But she will soon be with us by and by
We'll have to go to shop my love and get her favourite food
I bet she hasn't been eating like she should."
I could see they were excited and champing at the bit
So I walked back through the door and left them to it
When I told my other siblings they began to chaff
"What did you expect our Jen, it's kill the fatted calf."

SPOILT FOR CHOICE

HAS ANYONE EVER thought about the variety of fruit and veg
How a lovely orange pippin goes down well with a nice cheese wedge
With fresh baked bread and a slab of butter
Just the thing I hear you utter
A cooking apple scored and filled with raisins sweet
Roasted in the oven for a cold days treat.

I wander along the shelves in the supermarket store
There are fruits and veg of every sort galore
Exotic fruits, mundane fruits all displayed to tempt me
If I bought everything I saw my purse would soon be empty.

Peppers yellow, red and green
Like miniature pumpkins can be seen
Potatoes and onions so easily versatile
Catch my eye as I pause a while.

There's blueberries from Holland and Kiwi from New Zealand
And runner beans from Kenya in boxes on a stand
Star fruit, papaya and chinese lanterns too
Bananas, mango thus to name a few.

Carrots peas, cauliflower and the humble cabbage who
Juggle side by side with foreign fare on view
So many different fruit and veg from around the universe
It's hard to make a choice because they're so diverse
But in the end I must admit I'm governed by my purse.

HARVEST OF THE SEA

THERE ARE lots of creatures in the sea
Many unknown to you and me,
Some are large and some are small
But the sea by its size encompasses all.

We know of dolphins, whales and such
And sharks are talked of very much,
Porpoises leaping from the water with their shiny skin
Playing with their siblings very well akin
That they should always be on guard against a common foe
Which often lurks below.

Sometimes shoals of jellyfish are swimming by the shore
And many an unwary swimmer can be stung, it has been known before
Dead jellyfish can be seen stranded on the sand
Where the tide has swept them in with a contemptuous careless hand.

We know of pilchard, herring, and the common mackerel fish
Which when cooked make for a very tasty dish,
Haddock, place and turbot on the fishmongers slab
Cod, hake and salmon, whiting sole and dab
Are the common fish we know about just to name a few
And there are also other fish of every size and hue.

Some of the most dangerous are sea serpents and squid
For one never knows where they are hid,
The octopus with its tentacles can reach out to trap a man
And conger eels and electric eels are some of nature's plan
To make us all aware of the mighty power of the sea
And to treat it with caution, respect and very carefully.

FRIEND OR FOE

BY THE VERY NATURE of its being it is a complexity of art
And scientists are still working for its secrets to impart
But it covers two thirds of this global world
While we wait for its knowledge to be unfurled.

It can look so placid with its surface smooth but deep
But it can still make wives and children weep
When loved ones are lost while at their work
And plunged mercilessly beneath its murk.

For it can turn wild and stormy and is no one's friend
So don't expect it to unbend
Just to quench the general thirst
When it is deceiving and treacherous at its worst
It can lash the shores and islands with a ferocity so fierce
That even the best defences with its strength it can so pierce.

So it is best to treat with caution this element of power
And give it the respect it's earned for it will surely tower
Above some of natures offerings at any given hour
So if you're swimming, sailing, paddling or just walking on the sand
Don't forget the sea can play a very powerful hand.

KISMET

I'LL BE LOVING YOU ALWAYS is a tune I'll never forget
The band was playing it on the night that we met
I was eighteen and fancy free
He was just a little older than me.

We met in the interval through a cup of tea
Someone introduced us properly
After he tripped and spilt tea over my dress
And then apologised for causing me any distress.

And so we danced the night away in each other's arms
He was tall dark and handsome and I was smitten with his charms
He took me home and made a date for next day
And three weeks later we were engaged and thus our future lay.

And so the years sped quickly by
In the twinkling of an eye
We wonder where the years have gone
As we sit and dream and muse upon.

What might have been
If fate had not been kind to intervene
And bring us two together
To share our life we hoped for ever
And face what stormy weather came our way
And accept whatever fate before us lay.

THE CHOICE

JILL WAS HAVING HER BREAKFAST when the doorbell rang
She put her cup down and lightly sprang
To answer the summons and let her friend in
Who was looking very fashionably thin
And had called in to say
Not to forget it was a coffee morning today.

Jill offered her friend a cup of tea
Who accepted with alacrity
As her friend sipped the tea which was piping hot
For Jill always remembered to warm the pot
She looked on the table and saw something new
And as she gazed her curiosity grew
"I haven't seen that before," she said, surprise in her voice.

"No!" replied Jill. "I found I had a choice
What to do with Henry's ashes after the cremation
And after much deliberation
I thought well, he never worked while he lived with me
So I had them put in this smart egg timer that you can see."
And she looked at her friend and said, "More tea?"

THE WILLOWS

THE WILLOWS have their secrets as they sweep the river's banks
Hiding courting couples, watching youngsters pranks
And giving welcome cover on warm and sunny days
Inviting a cool shelter from the sun's strong rays.

The fronds of the willows droop low into the river
And when a wind springs up one can see the waters quiver
A punt can be seen floating 'neath the willows skirts
Bobbing gently up and down as though it lightly flirts
To vie for the attention of the river or a tree,
But it is tied fast and so it is not free
To make a decision on what is to be.

The moorhens and the swans use the willows for their shade
While they leave their nests where eggs are laid
Searching for insects and other repast
Their presence ever graceful as the river flows past.

A lone fisherman casts his line
Ever hopeful of a fish on which to dine
And so we leave the willows who seem to be on guard
For along the rivers banks for centuries they have starred.

A WOODLAND SCENE

WHEN THE SUN GOES DOWN the last streaks of red and
   coloured hues desert the sky
Nocturnal creatures stirring from their slumbers open a tentative eye
Old brock comes out to search for worms and grubs
Pushing his way through the undergrowth and shrubs.

The barn owl screeches as he searches for his prey
Swooping as he spies a mouse who is unable to get away
The hedgehog grunts and snuffles as it scuttles midst twigs and leaves
The dog fox sniffs the air as its nose it reeves.

The poacher sets his traps to see what he can catch
A plump rabbit for the pot perhaps or even a brace of pheasants may
   come up to scratch
But he has to look out for the game keeper in which he sometimes
   meets his match.

Everything has its order in Nature's way
All the different creatures by night and by day
Sharing the scene living side by side
Knowing when to be bold and when to hide
From an enemy or opportunist ready a meal to seek
For danger is ever present for the vulnerable and weak
And it seems that as soon as it is here the night is over
And the night time animals return to bed once again
To sleep through sunshine, snow and rain.

THE MISCHIEF MAKERS

THE WIND and rain joined forces together
   To show the strength of combining the weather,
They plotted and planned what mischief to make
Saying a temperate mood they would readily forsake
And said, "We'll cause so much disruption to everyday life
And give the nation some worry and strife."

"Who'll go first," they said to each other.
The wind said, "I will, my little brother."
He started to blow gently at first
Then harder and harder doing his worst.
He whipped the rivers 'til water covered the banks
For this was just the beginning of one of his pranks.

Dustbin lids clattered down alleys and streets,
He raced along the seafront and blew people off seats.
Their hats went whirling up to the sky
And much was the dust blown into many an eye.
The wind blew and blew until he'd blown himself out
He turned to the rain saying, "Turn and turn about."

So the heavens opened and down came the rain.
People ran for cover saying, "What a pain."
And people caught in the open searched for shelter in vain
Manholes were unable to cope with the flow
And pushed up the covers from the force below.
It spoilt peoples' picnics and garden fetes
For no one can predict the weather when they arrange their dates.

As suddenly as it started the rain ceased to fall
It turned to the wind and said, "Well brother
We've had such a good time we must do it again
But next time I think I'll go first," said the rain.
And the wind said in reply, "That's fine by me,"
So they both retired very happily.

THE COMFORT LADY

I'M WHAT IS KNOWN as a comfort lady
A profession which is often thought of as shady
But what do you do when you have no choice
And are a single mum without a voice
with not much income coming into the house
Irregular payments from my ex who's a louse.

I decided to setup a 'business' at home
So my kids would be safe and not left to roam
Yes! I'm a comfort lady, I don't advertise
I get regular guys.

My 'business' comes by word of mouth
My clientele are all over from north to south
I don't 'work' before or after school
For that is my golden rule
Holidays are sacrosanct
By then I've enough saved in the bank.

And when the children are old enough for me to leave
I have another card up my sleeve
I am taking a computer course and training to be on accountant
Then I can change my present mode of life and I won't be reluctant
To say goodbye to my clients and thank them for filling a gap
And you never know I might have some of them as my new clients mayhap.

DON'T SHOOT THE MESSENGER

WHY is it when you want to see the doctor of your choice
  They're never there or else booked up and you begin to voice
Your disappointment and dismay at being unsuccessful
At your attempt to get a time which makes it very stressful
You mutter imprecations and shake your fist at the telephone
And say "it's like trying to get blood from the proverbial stone".

But try to stop moaning and complaining and see the other point of view
That the doctors are ruled by the system and are often told what to do.
Too many pen pushers and not enough medical staff
If it wasn't so serious it would make a cat laugh.
The NHS isn't perfect, but better than that which we had.
For more lives are saved now of which we should be glad.
No, nothing is perfect it never was so,
Just count your blessings, even when spirits are low.

So if you can't get an appointment and disappointment is felt,
Put yourself in the doctors' shoes and the hand that they've been dealt
So don't shoot the messenger when you hear the receptionist say,
"I'm really sorry, there's nothing available today,
But try again tomorrow, it may be your lucky day".

FRESH START

IF YOU'VE LOST a loved one and are feeling rather sad,
  Just remember the good times and forget the bad
They are with you all the time in your mind's eye
To relive the happy hours of days gone by.

You can look at photo albums and see how it used to be
Re-read old letters and cards which stir the memory
And you'll find yourself smiling in spite of the pain in your heart.
No, don't forget the past but know there is a future
So give a mental shake of the head
And endeavour to make a fresh start.

THE PASSING OF AN OLD FRIEND

TODAY we mourn the passing
Of a dear and trusted friend
I fear we are not celebrating its untimely end.

This friend was always there you see
Through thick and thin to help me
But it seems it is old fashioned now
Where once it was used constantly.

This friend helped me through home work
And proved invaluable in my studies.
But now it seems it is only used by fuddy-duddies
It told me to look within
If the meaning was dim.

Good bye old friend my dictionary
To whom spelling once meant all.
Because today we are told
To be able to spell is not essential at all.

THE HUNTER HUNTED

THE SPARROW pecked the crumbs from off the lawn
The sun was warm on this Spring morn.
The hunter watched his prey with hooded eyes
As he hid in the bush he didn't realize
That he was stalked as well
By a large ginger tom without a bell
To announce a warning of the danger
From this domestic roaming ranger.

So the hawk sat blissfully unaware
His concentration so intense upon his future fare
Not knowing that he would receive his comeuppance
And that his life was not worth tuppence.
For the cat pounced upon the hawk
And the sparrow got away
To safety, and to live another day.

THE DANCE

M Y SISTER decided to go to one of the dances,
She'd been away for sometime and fancied her chances
She said, "We'll pull tonight or my names not Jane Brown."
So we dressed up to the nines and headed for town.

She said, "We'll try the Palais there's always plenty of talent there,"
So to look more sophisticated we put up our hair.
With pencil slim skirts and high heeled shoes.
We made our way humming the blues.

It was crowded in The Palais, more girls than men
Who because they were out numbered could easily
        pick and choose a partner and when
They eyed up the competition before they made their move,
Soon elbowing out the spotty and weedy youths
        for they had nothing to prove.

People said we were striking and easy on the eye,
So we didn't have any problem, my sister and I,
In getting a partner to circle the floor
My sister even attracted the attention of the bouncer on the door.

We met up in the interval and compared the partners we'd had
We had a marking system for dances,
Stars for the good and the bad
For some were better than others
And some we partnered were more like brothers
We decided to give these the cold shoulder
And dance with the ones who were bolder.

We both agreed when the evening was done
And we'd danced the last dance that we'd cut and run,
For we had a code my sister and I,
That we'd never leave the other high and dry
So when the band played the last waltz we caught each other's eye.
And when we finished dancing to our partners said good bye.

We rarely allowed them to escort us home especially after dark,
So we would arrange to meet them the next day in the local park.
Sometimes we turned up and sometimes we did not
Depending whether we liked them a little or a lot.
Sometimes we watched from a distance to see if they waited for us
If they weren't there my sister would shrug and say,
"Oh well there's always another bus."

SMILE

DON'T DESPAIR if you're feeling rather down
Put a smile on your face instead of a frown
And let it linger there for all to see
As you may get a smile back for a smile is free.

It costs nothing to brighten up another person's day
Plus you'll find that you'll feel better anyway.
And before you know it you'll begin to wonder why
That you ever felt so miserable that you wanted so to cry.
For a smile is like sunshine, it warms the very heart
And you'll find it is so easy once you start.

ARE YOU THERE

HELLO! Are you there?
I know you're in there somewhere
You used to be my parent my very lovely dad
Now you don't know me which makes me feel so sad.
You sit and stare and I say gently
    "Are you there?"

We used to have such happy times
My mum and you and I
But memories are all I have now
And they make me want to cry
You've such a lovely smile on your lined and care worn face
And I know that people say "there go us but for God's grace".

I hold your hand and stroke it
It makes me sad to see
That though you smile
You don't remember me
And I say in desperation and sheer frustration
    "Are you there?"

People say "I hope it isn't catching"
I reply "Its not like flu"
Anyone can get it, You, or you, or you.

I remember when at bed time you carried me upstair
And read a bed time story and then a special prayer
Helping with my home work and mending broken toys.
Giving me advice when I 'discovered' boys
When I was upset I sat upon your knee
You stroked my hair you were so loving to me.

When uncle Dave walked me up the aisle
I turned and you gave me your secret smile
You said you wouldn't give away your little girl
To any man as such
Because you loved me far too much.

At home I stare at your special place
Your empty chair
But your not there.

Bye bye dad see you next week
I feel so choked it's hard to speak
To an empty shell who used to be my dad
Who is not there.

FIRST LOVE

WHO COULD EXPLAIN this heady feeling
Which sent the very senses reeling
For she'd had no dealing with love before
Infatuation by the score.
But not this new lightheaded sensation
Where there was a sense of real elation
The spring in her step the lilt in her heart
This sudden bolt from cupid's dart.
                                        Oh! Joy.

She was in love there was no doubt
From the rooftops she wanted to shout
Her love aloud to all who'd listen
For in her eye a tear did glisten
Of pure happiness that this should be
And the glittering future she could see.

DESPERATION

I GO TO BED at night to sleep
But my problems come with me and though I know they'll keep
And that they should stay downstairs where they belong
They don't listen to me and come on strong.
I say to them "I need my rest, can't it wait until the morning please"
But they flit round and round inside my head with importunate ease
So I get up again and make a cup of tea.
But my problems keep me company
So I take a couple of sleeping pills and rest soon comes to me.

NOSTALGIA

WE USED TO WALK at the back of Dean Hall my family and I
　　Where rhododendrons grew near by
And daffodils trumpeted in the spring
A sight to make even a Philistine sing.

As we climbed the stile and entered the wood
A carpet of bluebells met our eye
And tall beeches reached toward the sky as if they should
Wind flowers nestled in the grass
Nodding and trembling as we did pass.

A spring ran across the path and disappeared among the trees
And fed a static pool which in the winter frosts would freeze
Where we, as children, spent many a happy hour sliding on the ice
Ignoring parents warnings and admonishing advice.

The grassy track on which we trod was flanked on either side
By hazelnut and chestnut trees where squirrels could easily hide
We shared the harvest with the squirrel when autumn time
　　came around
Where we would prise the nuts from the shells as they
　　lay upon the ground.
Oh the excitement of searching through the fallen leaves and
　　pricking tender fingers
I can still recall the earthy autumn scent as memory lingers
We emerged from the wood to an open plain where
　　blackberries grew aplenty
While we picked the luscious black fruit our old dog stood sentry.

Dean Hall is now a children's school, the path and wood no longer exist
And I mourn the passing of those wonderful moments lost in time's mist.
The pond now stagnant choked with weeds
All made way for children's needs,
No drill ground now where we played games
Where gypsies camped to further aims
All gone in the name of progress which makes me sad
And yet I have my memories, I should be glad.

We must move on and forward look
For we know authority will not brook
Any gentle sentiment to thwart their plan
From woman, child or any man.

As I reminisce once more
And open up another door
There are many rooms which feature in my past
And I know that all these memories will last
So I brush away the cobwebs that are lurking in my mind
To recall those childhood days which I have left behind.

MY NERVES AND ME

I LET MY NERVES get the better of me
They're with me from breakfast right through to tea
They're even with me when I go to sleep
When the sky is alive with stars that peep.

I wish there was a magic pill
That I could swallow at my will
To relax my nerves which plague me so
They're like the scales which go Doh Ray Doh.

My nerves are driving me round the bend
I certainly can't call them my best friend.
They pull my strings like I'm a puppet
Oh! Why oh why am I such a muppet.

THE WEDDING

THE WEEK BEFORE THE WEDDING the car hire firm rang
He didn't know if he would make it, the car had had a prang.
A bridesmaid had an accident riding pillion on a bike
There was uproar in the family, they'd never heard the like.

Another bridesmaid had started work and couldn't get away
She hoped it wouldn't spoil the day.
The best man wrote a letter to say he'd chickened out
He was very sorry but was sure someone else would step in no doubt.

So the groom asked another friend who said it was too much bother
In the end it was decided that the best man should be the groom's brother.

The night before the wedding a rehearsal was planned
Well, the car broke down, things were getting out of hand.
By the time the prospective pair arrived at the vicarage
The vicar said "No dice, see you in church tomorrow."
They felt despair had added to their age.

There was a petrol shortage at the time so the groom had hired a bus
To take the guests to church and reception without too much fuss.
Because there were so many children it was decided to keep the cost down
And restrict the number of guests which caused some parents to frown.
So half of them boycotted the wedding from annoyance and pique
They certainly didn't believe in turning the other cheek.
So the bus was completely empty only the driver at the wheel
So that was a waste of money and time and a poor deal.

When the reception was over and photos taken
The bride and the groom were surprised and shaken
When the groom's mother declared he should drive her back to her house
He gave in with good grace and didn't even grouse.

Three days into the honeymoon the husband went off to play darts
For when all's said and done he was a man of many parts
During the honeymoon the groom's nephews were taken ill
His mother was the person to call at will
Which left the bridesmaid with plastered leg to be looked after with the departure of her mother
So she joined the bride and groom
Which meant there were three on the honeymoon
The bride, the groom and one other.

Bride and groom have been together for over fifty years
Through laughter, pain and tears
The present mingling with the past
Who said it wouldn't last?

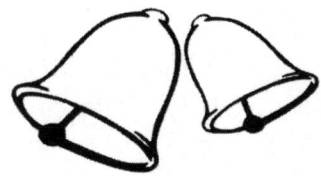

BITTER SWEET

I HAD A FATHER until I was four
Then one day he just walked out the door
My mother said, "We won't see him anymore."
I missed my father and couldn't understand why
He left my mother and me high and dry
I missed the laughter, the fun, the cuddles and the love
He used to call me his own little dove
When he left the joy went out of my heart
I never thought mother and he would part.

Mum went around with a face so worn and grey
She couldn't seem to motivate after he went away
I used to pray he would come back
For in my life I felt the lack
Of a father love to soothe my fears.

And so we managed through the years
And mum stopped shedding bitter tears,
Thus we moved on my mum and I
And closer we grew by and by
For mum and I closed ranks
We had little help so no one to whom we needed to give thanks.

I eventually married and had children on whom my mum doted
I said to her "don't spoil them" but there I was out voted
Poor mum she never really recovered from the shock
        when dad walked out
And the constantly struggling to make ends meet wore her down
        there is no doubt
Then she became ill and slowly sipped away
There were many tears I can tell you shed on that sad day.

One day a knock came on the door
A stranger stood upon the step and said,
"Don't you know me any more
I am your father, I wanted to see you once again
To say that I am sorry and I wanted to explain
Why I left you and your mother all those years ago
And I wanted to see my grandchildren I hear that I have now."
And a faint smile creased his brow.

I looked at him and replied, "The bible says you reap what you sow
I have no father, you lost that right thirty years ago
I'm afraid that you've left a re-union far too late,"
And I slammed the door and left him to his fate.

THE RELUCTANT SHOPPER

I SAW HIM in the supermarket bringing up the rear
This poor sad husband looking very drear.
He seemed resigned to following the trolley pushed by spouse
I am sure that he would rather be watching TV back at the house.

"Come along dear, keep up, and don't be slow.
Oh! Wait a minute, I've just seen Mrs So-and-So.
You know who I mean love, the one from number Ten
Oh dear! What was her name again?
My memory's really dreadful I must be getting old,
Her husband didn't answer, he wouldn't dare, he couldn't be so bold.

A quiet life was what he sought
He knew an argument would come to nought
Discretion being the better part of valour he held his tongue
And waited patiently until she'd done.
And knew that next week it would be the same again
For he wouldn't confess that he found it all a pain.
And so we'll leave him in the supermarket this lady's meekiish hubby
Wandering down the aisles, balding and a little tubby.

THE BITER BIT

I'M TIRED OF MY WIFE, In fact I'd like a fresh start
But I'm afraid I am a coward at heart
Plus she's the one with the money
And I'm not trying to be funny
When I say if I leave her I don't get a penny
Because I entered this marriage myself without any.

A germ of an idea is niggling in my mind
How to get rid of her and inherit the money she'll leave behind
I've heard there's a firm of 'removals' who
For a certain sum will know what to do.
I happened to mention this thought to a friend
Who said for a little consideration this problem he'd tend
But the actual contract would cost me much more.

So I meet the removal man away from my door
We agree on a price but I say I can't pay
Until the job is done and my wife's 'passed away'
The removal man considers this and decides to agree
Then says darkly, "But don't try to renege on the fee."

I tell my wife I'm going on a golfing weekend
And that I'll see her when I get back
I give her a Judas kiss on the cheek
As I go to the bedroom to pack.

I've arranged to meet up with a couple of mates
The hotel's quite cheap with reasonable rates
I would have stayed at the Club
But I'm afraid I'm behind with my sub.
That's another quirk of the wife, she's very mean with the readies
She'd rather spend her money on her hobby collecting teddies.

Well my alibi's fixed I can sit back and wait
For the news to come through that my wife's met her fate
On Saturday night there's a call from the Police
My wife's met with an accident can I come home please.

I return home suitably stressed
And looking carelessly dressed

I could see the young WPC was impressed
"Your wife's car left the road sir, and hit a tree
She didn't feel a thing, she died instantly."
I look very shocked and a tear leaves my eye.

The house seems empty without the wife
I think I'll sell it and start a new life.
It was a private funeral no flowers by request
Not many of us at the grave as she was laid to rest.

Then it's meet the solicitor for the reading of the will
He looks at me over his glasses, coughs, and I feel a slight chill
She'd made a new will alright, and it wasn't left to me
It seems she wasn't divorced when we wed
And that she had committed bigamy
All I get is a small legacy
The rest is left to charity.

Well, I can't pay the removal man that's for sure
I wish I'd known about her will before
For I know now what is the score.
I asked my friend to intercede on my behalf
He said I must be having a laugh
But he'd see what he could do.

Then the door bell goes, the grapevine has been busy
Suddenly I come over dizzy
I answer the door to see the removal man looking at me
He utters the words, "You reneged on my fee!"
Then he raises his gun and says,
"Have this one on me."

FILIAL DEVOTION

" THIS BLOOMING SAND gets everywhere," my mother said to me
She continued to grumble constantly
While she took off her shoes to shake the sand out
Standing on one leg looking pink and stout
She showed no gratitude,
In fact, I marvelled at her attitude
Then I remembered why she'd come
This largeish lumpy soul called mum
It was meant to take her mind off things
From all the problems that fate brings.

My family said it wouldn't work
I should have listened, I'm such a berk
She'll never change they all commented
The more you do the more demented
You will become by taking mum.
"Don't say we didn't give you warning,"
They all cho700sed on the morning
As we set off, me feeling optimistic
Accepting my share of things domestic.

She decided to visit the fairground
But found the attractions quite tame
"We'll try the big Dipper," she said
And I wished that we'd never came.
We climbed steadily to the top
Then plunged to a gut wrenching drop
I left my stomach behind
When we got to the bottom I looked at my mother
And my thoughts were not kind.

From then on things gradually started going downhill
By the end of the day I felt quite ill
I was glad to get my mum back home
Perhaps next time we'll try the Millennium Dome.

TIME WITH MUM

" COME ALONG," mummy said "It's time for your bath."
As she scooped me up clearing toys from her path.
"The water's nice and warm," she said.
"And when you've finished it will be time for bed."

She lowers me gently and washes my hair
She washes me tenderly with loving care
Mummy never gets the soap in my eyes
For she's the bestest mummy and ever so wise.

The soap bubbles get up my nose
They make me sneeze right down to my toes
"Can I have Teddy?" I ask with a grin
And when he is passed to me I drop him in.

When mum lifts me out Ted's as wet as me
I giggle and chuckle with childish glee
I'm wrapped in a lovely warm towel from the rail
But poor Ted is left on the rack looking pale.

Mummy reads me a story when tucked in my bed
And when she's finished this prayer is said
Angels guard you round your bed
Two at the foot and two at the head.

Mummy says,
"Tuck down, Mr. Sandman's on his way
For tomorrow is another day."
The last thing I see is mum smiling at me
As I drift into sleep so contentedly.

THE CHRISTMAS PRESENTS

THANK YOU DEAR for my lovely warm bedsocks
When I expected a diamond ring with stones as big as rocks
And that fluffy bright scarf
I thought you must be having a laugh.
When I saw all that tissue beckoning me
I thought a welcome mink stole I should see
As I opened the present I brushed away a tear
It will go with the others that you've given me year after year.

And the jeweller's box with the long slender shape
A pearl necklace at least with a silver fastener to clasp at my nape
But what did I find when I looked inside
A new watch strap you said for
My old one was looking sad and unkind.

Another present? I thought this must be the one
As a fragrant aroma wafted my way
My favourite perfume will make my day
But what was revealed to my disbelieving eyes
Was a bottle of bath salts to my surprise
I smiled sweetly and said, "Thank you dear and
Would you like to open your presents now?"

"What! You don't care for the present I bought you," I said
"A new table lamp for the side of your bed
You complained that the old one was looking shabby and worn
Now now dear don't look so forlorn."

"For you've another present or two to explore
One a men only magazine over which you can pore
And the tool box I bought especially for you
Is it not to your liking you look a shade blue."

"I'm sorry if you're disappointed
I thought the presents well appointed
Never mind there's always next year
And a Merry Christmas to you as well my dear!"

REFLECTIONS

THEY SAY to every thing there is a season
But we wonder sometimes for what rhyme or reason.
In the spring new baby lambs are born
In the summer sheeps' coats are shorn
The sun's warmth and soft falling rain
Speeds the growth of the crops and swells the grain.

In the autumn leaves fall from the trees
Encouraged by a strengthening breeze
Leaving the branches bare and stark
Ready to greet winter's evening dark.

Snow falls gently to the ground
Like a blanket with its arms around
To cover and protect new life hidden below
Until spring comes again when snow melts and streams and rivers flow
To breathe new life as nature opens yet another door.
And so another year begins and the cycle repeats itself once more
And we are left to marvel at the wonders which we see
That nature bequeaths to us for all eternity.

PITTER PATTER

PITTER PATTER goes the rain
Running down the window pane
Bouncing off the window ledge
Onto ground along lawn's edge
Soaking grass and borders too.

Rain drops falling from shrubs and trees
As nature holds her breath waiting for the rain to cease
Suddenly there's a break in the cloud
The sun comes out looking pleased and proud.

Steam rises from the roads now drying
A rainbow appears now the rain has stopped crying
The chill in the air from the shower of rain
Is now damp and humid in the main
And our English climate which can amaze
Is the topic of conversation on most days.

DESTINY

SHE TRIPPED DOWN the street
Ready to meet
    Her Destiny.

Her high heeled shoes went clickety clack
Beating a tattoo on the pavement stones
The night was so cold it chilled the bones
As she went to greet
    Her Destiny.

He said he would come tonight
She needed the money for things were tight
She had never done anything like this before
And wondered if she should have asked for more
As she went to face
    Her Destiny.

He stood in the shadows and a silk scarf he fingered
He was alone, no other soul lingered
She came to the appointed place
And called, "Are you there?"
As the moon slid from behind a cloud
He caught a glimpse of her pale face
And nervous stare.

He whispered, "Over here"
And as she came near
He slipped the silk scarf around her neck and pulled it tight.
She had no time to fight
Or regret the reason why she came
For blackmail is a dangerous game
And for this she met
    Her Destiny.

THE CHAIR

I AM A CHAIR
Not any old chair so there
I'm not a kitchen or dining room chair
For anybody to plank their derriere
    I'm Special
I am the chair.

I am placed in the entrance of a very large hall
For important people to sit when they call
While they wait for their host to welcome them in
For it is quiet and restful away from the din
Of the many activities carried out within
    For I'm Special
I am the chair.

I am polished and buffed to the highest degree
They take very good care of me
    For I'm special
I am the chair.

I sit where I am for a good many years
Then hard times hit the hall and it ends in tears
My master has lost all his money I'm told
And everything in the house has to be sold.

I wonder what will happen to me
I'll have a new master but I'll not worry
For I'm special you see
    I am the chair.

THE WOMAN AT THE GATE

SHE LEANS ON THE GATE with a cigarette between her fingers
While all around her the aroma of poverty lingers
With her thin scrawny figure
She was never much bigger
She looks a poor tired thing
I wonder if she regrets the symbolic wedding ring.

With her straggling eldritch locks
And shabby washed out frocks
She is the epitome of constant struggling
To make ends meet and is forever juggling
To stretch her meagre house keeping
And try to keep her soul from weeping
As she tends for her husband and family
Living very frugally.

What happened to the pretty young girl
Who was so gay with a carefree air
With bright blue eyes and burnished hair
With smooth complexion once so fair.

Now with work worn hands and a defeated manner
She wears her weariness like a banner
For the future looks bleak
Not much hope at the end of each week
Perhaps in time the future will bring
More happier days when she can laugh again and sing.

THE CLUB

IDIDN'T WANT to join this club
It's not exclusive nor confined to the pub
There are so many of us
We're a threat to the powers that be
They say that we cost too much no doubt
We're a burden they could do without
And they'd like us to disappear you see.

For we are the grey haired brigade
We're on parade
For a better style of living
We're tired of hand outs from the state
Whenever it feels like giving.

We soldier on spending what savings we've got
For there's little help if they think you've a lot
Bureaucracy meddles and governs our life
Leaving us struggling with stresses and strife.

We've contributed to this nation's wealth
When we most need help we are taxed by stealth
We were told to save for our old age
So we did our best and now find our savings
Eroded and dwindling at every stage.

My advice to the youth of today
Is don't bother to save, in fact why bother to work
Your responsibilities you might as well shirk
Or you'll end up like us worn out and tired
From caring for others and now we've retired
We can't get away
From the problems and worries of every day.

THE VIOLETS

DAD WAS TAKEN ILL one day
And went to the hospital for quite a long stay
When he got to the hospital he looked very sickly
And the surgeon decided to act quite quickly
It was touch and go the surgeon said to mum
Who was so shocked she was struck dumb
Dad wasn't allowed to have worries or cares
As he rested in hospital at the top of the stairs.

Mum and I went to see him once a week
She told him everything was fine with a peck on his cheek
We struggled to live on a weekly income from the
     National Assistance Board
The princely sum of thirty bob with nothing left over to hoard
I was thirteen at the time and mum and I were on our own.

But neither of us thought to moan
We soldiered on putting on a brave face
We lived on bread and jam, nothing fancy at our place
I was entitled to free school dinners but I couldn't face the shame.
So mum parted with half a crown so things would look the same.

I marvelled at my mother as she smiled and talked to dad
Hiding all our problems not letting him know that things were bad
My mother and I clung together, the outside world didn't know
For we closed ranks so nothing would show
We were very lonely mum and I and lived behind a mask
No one offered to help and mum was too proud to ask.

Then as we were coming home one day from visiting my dad
Feeling rather low and a little bit sad
We saw a flower seller in the town
I gazed at the violets she held in her hand
Who looked at me and said, "Aren't they grand?"
Mum saw the longing in my eyes
And she bought them much to my surprise
With a precious sixpence which she could ill afford
She handed me the violets over which I'd pored.

She said, "You've been such a good girl these last few weeks."
The colour flew up into my cheeks
"You've never complained or grumbled at all
You shall have your violets although it's something small."

Then suddenly the sun came out as we made our way home together
And we smiled at each other as we walked arm in arm
For we made these trips whatever the weather
I am old now but I've never forgotten that loving gesture
From a wonderful mum who made sacrifices through that very bleak year
And how we relied upon each other as I wipe away a tear.

THE CHASE

THE HUNTSMEN MEET on a morning bright
A colourful sight to behold
The master's quaffed the stirrup cup
The horses paw the frost hard ground
When the fox is soon in sight.

The hounds give chase eager and bold
Baying in the crisp cold air
The sun struggles through with a watery smile
Promising a day to be fair.
Tally Ho! and away they go
The hunt supporters juggle side by side
With the anti-sports brigade who will not be decried.

The riders in pink go galloping on
The huntsman's horn sounds clear and strong
Music to the ears of the following throng.
A low stone wall skirts the edge of the field
The fox jumps it unwilling to yield
His life for the huntsmen's idea of fun
For the chase is still on and not yet done
He wades through a stream to cover any track
To throw off the scent of the hollering pack
For old Reynard is wily and has been here before
He knows all the dodges and what is the score.

Suddenly the hounds stop running
They mill around for they're not funning
They've temporarily lost the scent of the fox
Who's at a safe distance and quietly mocks
At the confusion and melee he's left in his wake
And the frustrated cries the riders make
But suddenly the hounds pick up the trail again
And they're off like greased lighting no one can restrain.

There's a shout from the riders, a horse has gone lame
A rider's been thrown. Oh dear! what a shame
But they can't hang about while the hunt's in full cry
So it's on with the chase while spirits are high.

But Reynard's had enough of the dodging and weaving
He's breathing hard and his flanks are heaving
He decides to end this tiring chase
And head for the woods where he has his base
Deep below brambles which cover the ground
So densely packed no lair could be found
A bramble thicket is best left alone
The chase is over for this day at least
As the Master calls off the hunt for the beast
They've had a run for their money and head back for home
No blooding today for the newest member
Just an enjoyable day to remember.

When the dust has settled old Reynard will roam
To plunder hen houses causing havoc and stress
Scattering feathers, disturbing the nests
Chickens clucking and squawking running hither and thither
This place and that all in a dither.

But its not just chickens, baby lambs are not free
From the predator's forays carried out with much glee
For the fox is heartless, no compassion has he
For all the heartache he causes and the misery.
And that is why he is hunted all over the land
To prevent destruction getting out of hand
But for this once he appears to have won
Though he needs to watch out for the farmer's gun
For it's a long running battle between fox and man
For each will try to out wit the other if he can.

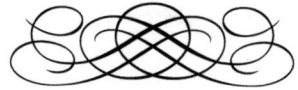

SHAVERS AND QUAVERS

HAVE YOU EVER joined a choir or singing group
Were you at the front or back while they all trooped
Into church or village hall
Where they belted out their all
And did it leave you feeling Cock-a-hoop?

Poor Richard is tone deaf
Doesn't know a quaver from a clef
Which leaves the conductor quite bereft of speech
He's tried and tried with Richard
And thought that he could reach
Some inner core of music from the lad
But for now he shrugs his shoulder
For young Richard's getting bolder
And thinks that he's as good as his old dad.

Some people leave their best until the last
They like the audience to hear a vocal blast
There is always one who'll shout
Who's convinced there is no doubt
For he's the one who's nailed his colours to the mast.

The conductor gives him quite a steely glare
The culprit just gives back a stare for stare
For he is blissfully unaware
That he's the one at fault
And the conductor sighs
For his glare has come to nought.

But for now we'll leave them struggling
As the conductor does the juggling
With a motley crew of old and young alike

For when you sum it up
Who wants to win a cup?
The taking part is what it's all about.

THE SPECIALIST

I GET UP IN THE MORNING and drag myself downstairs
It really is an effort
For I feel that no one cares.

I went to see a specialist about my tale of woe
How my legs turn to jelly
But he didn't want to know
He sat there grim, forbidding
As he barked and growled at me
And I felt so very helpless
For he showed no sympathy
For my sorry plight
And I felt quite quite
As though I could smack his head
For being so obtuse when my legs they feel like lead.

I came away from my consultation
My whole being filled with frustration
For I'd failed to get my message across
And I felt my cause was really lost
If we could change places and he felt my pain and grief
He'd soon find a solution and then I'd obtain some relief.

FALSE ALARM

THANK YOU DOCTOR for coming in the night
When I thought I'd had a heart attack
And given myself a fright.
'Twas only indigestion was what to me you said
How was I to know it was from eating too fresh bread.

A FRIEND

A FRIEND is always there for you
No matter if you're feeling blue
A friend is there in foul or fair weather
You'll feel you'll always be together
A friend will always come up trumps
Especially when you've got the hump.

The sink's blocked up, you've broken a nail
You've got a migraine and looking pale
The cat's been sick on your husband's shirt
Who's screaming the place down
You'ld thought he'd been hurt.

The washing machine's broken down again
The plumber can't come and it's starting to rain
Your offspring want to stay off school
They always think that they can fool
An old hand like yourself whose been this way before
You don't fall for it and push them through the door.

You think shall I light a cigarette and toss back a sherry
Oh! What the heck let me be merry
Who's that coming up the path
Why it's my friend, we're bound to have a laugh
For a friend in need is a friend indeed
You've found this to be true
Especially when your tearing your hair and feeling very blue.

A friend is better than cigs and drink
You suddenly feel fine and in the pink
The sun's come out hip hip hooray
We'll banish the blues for another day.

THE PARTING

" I WANT TO COME HOME with you" she cried
This heartrending cry came straight from the heart
As she twined her arms around his neck
He knew they would soon have to part.

He gave a huge sigh as he hugged her back
And a tear glistened in his eye.
He felt really saddened as he held her close
For this was another goodbye.

Just one of the many they had to endure
His daughter and he
Because of a ruling passed last year by the court
For that is the price an estranged parent pays
When he and his ex-partner go separate ways.

THE EASTER TREAT

H AS THE EASTER BUNNY been to visit you
With an extra large chocolate egg or two
Decorated with flowers and your name in icing sweet
You can indulge for once in this very special treat.

For Easter is like Christmas, it comes but once a year.
So go on spoil yourself for you know that it will cheer
The very cockles of your heart
And when you have finished you can always start
Your diet tomorrow or even in the next few weeks
Just savour the chocolate for now which is bulging out your cheeks.

DEJA VU

THEY GATHERED on street corners these army of men
Dressed in the same uniform of caps/mufflers, shabby suits and when
They looked at passers by all hope evaporated from sunken eyes
Which couldn't even reach towards the skies
Saving woodbine ends in battered tins which had seen better days
While the aura of poverty hung in the air with a dismal haze.

Scavenging the ash tips for cinders to sell from door to door
Two pence a bucket to those who weren't so poor
Who took pity on these desperate folk
With no sign of work and just plain broke
In spirit as well as pocket it hit the nation hard
For this was the Depression with No holds barred.

Who could forget the days of bread and dripping
Where hopes of a better future were slipping
When the miners went on strike their slogan was
Not a penny off the pay not a minute on the day
Their case was doomed it was heard to say
And so it proved for they went back achieving nowt
And for some it meant a permanent lock out.

For they were classed as trouble makers and were turned away from work
And the employers in their triumph did not hesitate to shirk
To call them militants and communists and sometimes even worse
And the unfortunate concerned lived a long time with this curse
And so we've turned full circle for a recession has struck again
But now it's called the credit crunch causing misery and pain.
They say that it will last at least another twenty years
Leaving people gazing sadly into many an empty purse
But we pray that from this fiasco a valuable lesson will be learned
And try to prevent in future not to get our fingers burned.
We must remember the past that when Pandorar's box was opened
Hope was what remained
So hope is what we must all cling to for a secure future to be regained.

THE CALENDAR

THE CALENDAR has moved from week to week
Sometimes I think that it can really speak
To remind me when appointments made are due
And even birthdays and anniversaries too.

For the calendar waits for no man like time and tide I fear
It goes on inexorably 'til the end of another year.
So don't procrastinate over things that should be done
Or you'll find another year has gone and the calendar has won.

THE DOLLY MOP

SHE STANDS on the street corner
Her budding breasts straining against her skimpy top
Short skirt, knee length boots, her hair a frizzy mop.
Stating, "I'm here to be laid
For such is my trade"
And of her young body a predator will raid.

Sixteen, seventeen, not much older
Looking pinched around the mouth as the weather turns colder
Feeling nervous but trying to look bolder.

Along comes her pimp with a scowl on his face
She's not earning enough so has fallen from grace
He pinches her arms 'til they're black and blue
And says, "Work harder or it will be the worse for you".

I feel for her, I really do
She'll probably end up diseased or maimed
For she's a victim, more to be pitied than blamed.

THE JOYS OF PARENTHOOD

WHO'D HAVE children?
From birth they're geared to irritate
Their parents programmes they frustrate
But now you've got them it's too late
To change your mind.

Who was it went all quiet and broody?
Feeling temperamental and moody
Whose bright idea was this we say
They change your life that's for sure
And as for wealth they keep you poor
Forever and a day.

As soon as that baby comes into your home
It's got the upper hand
Who said that babies sleep for hours
They certainly never had one like ours
Who thought that night was made for play
And we'd be hollow eyed next day.

An old wives' saying goes like this
When babes are small your arms will ache
When they grow up your heart will break
So raising them is not all bliss.

As they get older things should improve
But they're deceitful and cunning and planning their next move
We'll take them to granny's parents say with relish
For surely grandparents will want to cherish
The little darlings they hope and pray
But how strange, granny seems to be out that day.

At last they are five and off to school
And there the teacher will over rule
Self willed and naughty attributes
And cut down to size those too big for their boots.

And so the years just roll on by
Some times you laugh and some times cry
At antics droll or just plain daft
While your wallet goes on feeling the draught.

You've got through sports days fund raising and Christmas nativities
Plus all the extras labelled activities
The long school holidays which never seem to end
Teachers rest and mothers worry
Enough to drive you round the bend.

They're chauffeured here and chauffeured there
When have you got time to spare
To follow your hobbies and have leisure
Or even indulge in a little pleasure.

CD, TV blaring half the night
Neighbours banging on the wall their attitude uptight
Hogging the phone when it's you that pay the bills
Hearing "Don't use the phone mum I'm expecting a call from the Wills"
Borrowing the car because they can't afford their own
Teenage years are heart sink years
When all you do is seem to groan.

The teenage years have come and gone
You've given them a shoulder to cry upon
Tears and tantrums broken romances
You've seen it all so what are the chances
They'll learn by their mistakes and not do it again
But that's what growing up is sunshine after rain.

But when they grow up and leave the nest
What are you going to do with all that rest
But don't be too hasty and don't jump the gun
Your real worries have just begun
We cant lead their lives for them
Although we may try
As we see their mistakes and heave a huge sigh.

We find it hard to let go
As we wait in the wings
For it's a toss up who'll cut the apron strings
But we're getting older and don't want the stress
Of offsprings' problems which never get less.

And now we have grandchildren from the seeds which we've sown
We see the dangers we never saw with our own
And as they visit and want to play
That's when we realise why granny was out that day.

DOMESTIC STRIFE

MUMMY AND DADDY are at it again
I never know when
To ask for a hug
They look at me and their shoulders they shrug.

I wish they'd stop I can't stand this noise
I think I'll go into the garden and play with my toys
Mummy's crying, dad has hit her I think
He always does this when he's had too much drink.

It's gone very cold I'll put on my coat
Daddy's got mummy' round the throat
Now Mummy's lying on the floor
I gaze at the scene from the door.

Daddy's eyes are wild, his hair all askew
I look at him, I don't know what to do
Suddenly Mum lets out a moan and her eyes open wide
So I sidle further inside.

Then she looks at Dad and he picks her up
And holds her close to his chest
He kisses her face and strokes her hair
While her tears are soaking his vest.

Then without a word they reach out to me
And I'm held in a warm embrace
1'm part of the circle, I sigh with relief
It shows all over my face.

I know it won't last for it's happened before
And it will happen again sometime
But until that occurs I'll accept what is now
And just take one day at a time.

INTROSPECTIVE

FOLLOW YOUR HEART and not your head
How many times has this been said?
It's easy to be practical and follow a single course
And try reasoning from every source.

Why let people quash your dreams
'Til your hopes and desires fade away
Stand up for yourself and be counted
And then you may win the day.

Aspirations, hopes and fears
Which follow us down throughout the years
Some days full of sunshine
Some days marked by tears.

The flotsam and jetsam of every soul
Can be found tossed in one large mixing bowl
But we're all individuals and must remember as such
On recognising this we can achieve much.

ON THE RUN

I SEE they're still searching for me
'Famous Doctor' on the run
Will the fools never give up
Wishing to punish me for my excesses of fun.

So my genetic experiments
Caused a few freaks
To be unleashed on an unsuspecting world
Resulting in shrieks
Of horror, disgust and other reactions.
So I got a few sums wrong
I was never good at fractions.

They called me Dr. Frankenstein
A man much underrated
A product of a fertile mind
And sad to say out dated.

I did what I had to do
Because I was under orders
I didn't wish to be carried off
Between two stolid warders.

Spending my days in a punishment cell
Or something probably worse
For the man at the top was impatient
And would only rant and curse
If results were not fast.

But it's all in the past
Who wants to remember
Why rake up the ashes
And stir the dead embers
Of things best forgotten
Just leave me be
In a world that is rotten.

SAUCE FOR THE GOOSE

WE HAD BEEN TOGETHER a very long time
The wife and I
And thought it would last forever
Who would have thought she'd up and leave
While I vainly tried to endeavour
To fathom the reason she suddenly left
Leaving me feeling so utterly bereft.

My wife was attractive and tidy and smart
And also so very dear to my heart
She said she'd outgrown me and was moving on
And said all the romance had literally gone
From our marriage.

And she felt like a change
She was looking for someone
More top of the range
And younger to boot
She'd found someone to suit.

So this was goodbye
Leaving me high and dry
Or so she thought.

Now she has left my life
I can start over again
With a dear little dolly bird
Called Elizabeth Jane.

THE EMPIRE

WHEN QUEEN VICTORIA was on the throne
We had an empire which had grown
To cover two thirds of the world at least
Missionaries and explorers taming man and beast.

We could look at the atlas and where we saw areas shaded in pink
We knew that was ours but now our hearts sink.
For the empire has shrunk beyond recognition
And the music hall artistes who gave a rendition
Extolling the virtues of the territories we held
Would be hard put to praise what is left to us now
For the Lion's had his teeth drawn, and how.

Now the Great has been taken out of Britain which has gone to the dogs
So is it worthwhile still oiling the cogs
Of a mechanism misused and let down.
Who's responsible we ask, was it politician or clown
Were they sadly misguided, this we must stress
For they have left us in a terrible mess.

WHAT PRICE JUSTICE

WHAT PRICE 'JUSTICE' which is meted out today
To criminals who stab and shoot our young leaving families in disarray.
The judges eyes seem blinkered
As with sentences they've tinkered
Which is loaded in the offenders favour so some say.

Should the punishment fit the crime is sometimes asked
By people who despair when they see the guilty have basked
In the glory of publicity and 'the cachet' they've achieved
By beating the system not caring who is grieved.

For 'Justice' needs a shake up of that there is no doubt
It should be tougher not softer for the scales to balance out
And so we wait in the wings to see what will occur
Well you never know things might change next year.

ENVY

WHY IS IT THAT EVERYTHING you touch turns to gold?
While my attempts end in dross
I'm at a loss
To understand why
Is it because you're more bold than I?

We bought the same shares and backed the same horse
I sold my shares too early of course
I put a small bet on the horse that we chose
I backed him each way I'm afraid
While you put a small fortune and backed him to win
That's why your winnings were larger than mine I suppose
And that's why I guess you're quids in.

Why is it that I never get things right
Why do I feel that I have to fight
For my share of good fortune and luck
For you hardly lift a finger to earn a quick buck
And you've got a better job in the city than me
While I'm still in a rut more's the pity you see.

Shall we ever be equal I say to myself
Although I don't hold out much hope
So I'll struggle on and do my best to cope
With this feeling of envy which fills my mind
And try to catch up because I'm way behind.

MY GRAN

MY GRAN HAD ARTHRITIS quite badly in her legs
And was very shaky on her old pegs
One leg was worse than the other
She confided in my mother
And was off to the doctor's for him to take a look.

She finished work with a bit of a scurry
So, no time to wash both legs for she was in a hurry
She didn't want to miss the bus
And couldn't understand why mum should fuss
When gran said she'd only time to wash one leg
He was only going to look at one
When all was said and done.

When she arrived home my mother asked how she got on
My gran said sheepishly, "He looked at both my legs."
My mum said, "Told you so" from the armchair she was sat upon.
Now when we go to the doctors the family all chant
"Don't forget to wash both legs," and we call back, "We shan't".

A PARENT'S GRIEF

IF YOU HAVEN'T LOST A CHILD you will never understand
The savage tearing of the heart by fate's untimely hand
We never have them long enough we feel with some despair
Who can explain the hurt and pain which fills the very air.

The memory of a child's laughter and tears
Stays with one hauntingly down through the years
The pitiful nosegays laid on the grave
A constant reminder while we try to be brave
To get through the days which are hollow and bleak
Shall we ever come to terms with it we wonder every week.

But we have to make that effort for the ones who love us so
For they support us gladly of this we know
In time perhaps the pain may dull but the ache will still be there
So we'll put a smile on our face for the world not to see
This sadness which we bear.

WHAT WILL HAPPEN TO ME?

I DON'T WANT to grow old,
I feel full of despair.
What will happen to me
When I can't climb the stair?
"You'll be put out grass"
I am told cheerfully
But when I can't 'chew the cud'
What will happen to me?

"We'll find a good home
You'll get care and attention"
'They' don't ask if I want to
'They' don't even mention
An alternative choice
I daren't even plea
What will happen to me?

Their faces will harden
Excuses run rampant
Like weeds in a garden
"We haven't the room"
"We aren't qualified nurses"
And if I turn mulish
I'll bring down their cures
Upon my frail head.

My eyes fill with tears
I feel full of self pity
Oh! Dear Lord
What will become of me?

HANDS ACROSS THE SEA

ON THE 7th of December 1941
The Japs bombed Pearl Harbour diving from the sun
Tora! Tora! Tora! was the cry from the skies
And people tried to take cover amid panic and cries.

This blatant attack was a shock to the yanks
Who had given much thanks
To be kept from the war
And soon Europe was invaded
With gum chewing Joe's, Chuck's and Hank's
Who were very upset to be dragged in once more
To take part in the fight of a Second World War
And there was many an antagonist
Towards Hitler the protagonist.

On February 15th 1942 Singapore fell to the Japs
Who had come in 'the back way' through jungle on bicycle and foot
Which caught everyone napping especially the official chaps
Too late to escape for many left behind
Who faced the enemy proudly and hoped they would be kind
To the sick and disabled in a hospital bed
But found to their dismay they were bayoneted instead.

When the Americans landed on our shore
It changed many lives that's for sure.
Amongst the children there was great excitement
But amongst some adults there was much resentment
Over paid, over sexed and over here
Was the common cry poured into the ear
While the Americans on their part complained of warm beer.

The friendly Americans weren't used to the British reserve
Who thought the Yanks brash with plenty of nerve
But the Americans showed they could be generous too
Which the British soon found to be true
They were strangers far from their native land
Feeling uprooted, missing their families and everything familiar to hand
They were grateful for kindnesses shown by us
Who took them into our homes and sometimes into our hearts
without too much fuss.

The Americans from down South said, "Don't call us damn Yanks
For if you do you'll get no thanks"
As there was still rivalry between South and North
For the Civil war was still fresh in their minds
At how the Generals had sallied forth
To fight the Yanks who Johnny Reb hated.
You'ld have thought by now that feelings had abated.
But they had to join forces to fight this new threat
And to remind us how much we were in their debt.

When they arrived they brought colour and cheer
And brightened an austere war while they were here
They were kind to the children giving Christmas parties
        and hiring a cinema for a special showing
And when it was time to leave gave them presents which
        left their faces glowing.

They charmed the British girls with their good manners, nylons and treats
And what they called candy and we called sweets
Which resulted in the weddings and after the war
The girls sailed across the sea as GI Brides away from the British shore.

While the British boys grumbled that the Yanks had taken the best
And they voiced their resentment which burned in their breast
I was a child during the war and the Americans were very kind to me
Generous with their time and very friendly.
They left as they suddenly came
To finish what was started as this wasn't a game
We missed them for a while but life goes on
Leaving us with memories to muse upon.

I REMEMBER

I REMEMBER when as children
How we laughed and sang and played
We wandered through the woods all day
In sunshine and in shade.

We never minded if it rained
Or when the wind blew cool
For the forest was our playground
Over which we all did rule.

Thus felt as children often do
With the arrogance of youth
And never thought ourselves
As anything but couth.

I remember when the countryside
Was blanketed in snow
And the pond was frozen over
When the water ceased to flow.

How we slipped and slid and slithered
As we stumbled on the ice
Our noses red as cherries
Which wasn't very nice.
Our shoes and socks were sodden
From contact with the snow
But we didn't care, for we were young
And always on the go.

How we laughed to see our poor old dog
As he skittered in our wake
'Twas a comical sight with his legs splayed out
As he suffered for our sake.

I remember when at Christmas time
We gathered round the fire
Making decorations of which we never seemed to tire
Christmas cards, calendars and chinese lanterns too
The kitchen table littered with scissors, brush and glue.

We dutifully wrote to Santa
Letters full of hope
Which we 'posted' up the chimney
Not caring how he'd cope.

And so to bed excited as we scurried up the stairs
And clambered in between the sheets
To say our nightly prayers.
We always had a bedroom fire
To keep the cold at bay
What a warm and cheerful sight
At the end of a winter's day.

I remember the firelight
Flickering on the walls
Dancing on the ceiling
The memory never palls.

We struggled hard to keep awake
As we chatted to each other
But sleep soon overcame us
To the amusement of our mother.

At last it was Christmas morning
We woke up before it was light
The fire was dead, the room gone cool
But we were feeling happy and bright.

We felt down the bed to see if Santa had been
We found our stockings but they seemed a bit lean
The older one said, with a laugh in her voice,
"Don't you know there's a war on
And they hadn't much choice?"

I remember going up to bed one balmy summer's eve
As I glanced through the landing window
I could hardly quite believe
The sight of a handsome fox slinking toward the farm
Preparing to raid the hen house
Meaning to do them harm
To provide for his family was his intent
Toward this end the fox was bent.

I remember my sister dressed as a witch
Taking our tom cat
Using improvisation, she was very good at that
The blackout material a perfect disguise
For the fancy dress comp, for she won second prize.
She came home triumphant as she showed us the money
Her success feeling as sweet as honey.

I remember going blackberrying with mother and with gran
The spiky brambles spread out like a fan
Mum said, "Be careful where you step."
Too late there was a cry
My gran had overbalanced
And gave us a smile quite wry.

Each year my cousin helped to build a fire for bonfire night
And when it was time to light it
Hid beneath the bed in fright.

So many memories as they juggle for supremacy
The laughter joy and tears which are part of children's legacy
They linger in the background as we move on down the years
An occurrence happens and our memory stirs.
I find there is pleasure and also pain
As I travel back in time down memory lane.

LOOKING BACK

DO YOU REMEMBER Babycham with the cherry on a stick,
We sipped it slowly, we weren't meant to drink it quick,
We had to respect the boyfriend's means for the wages. were not high.
And we'd sit looking into each other's eyes while time slipped by.
There was no eating out at posh hotels
Just transport caffs and fish and chips.
And a walk through forest dells.

We'd go to the flicks on a Saturday night
And grumble if someone came in late
While the usherette flashed a light
For when you stood up a trampled foot could be your fate.
We'd have an ice cream in the interval and perhaps a box of chocs
The girls wore stiletto heels and nylons adorned with 'clocks'. *

We sometimes went to a dance at the Miners Hall
Where we danced with the fellas, some short, some tall.
We used to meet in Merediths caff
Where we had a coffee and a laugh
The soundproof booth in the music shop was always a draw
Where we listened to the latest record with awe.

We cycled through the lanes on sunny days
The exuberance of youth like a golden haze.
We ran for buses in wind and rain,
And got a 'stitch' for our pain,
We went for a ramble 'over the rocks' to Soudley on summer evenings fair
For we were young and healthy and didn't have a care.

Who could forget the Coffee Tavern on the other side of the Dean
Where the young could be seen
And the Lawrence's faggots and peas
Always guaranteed to please
Plus the short cut through the Angel opposite the Town Hall and marketplace.
But sadly now Town Hall and Market place have gone
And of the short cut there is no trace
For the Angel owners blocked it off
To preserve their private face.

As I cope with my Fibromyalgia
I look back on the past with nostalgia
My husband says, and it's perfectly true
That no-one can take the memories away from you.

* Embroidered motif

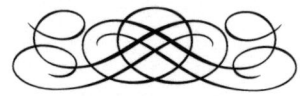

www.fineleaf.co.uk